We Chose Life
Why You Should Too

By Anthony Horvath

ATHANATOS
PUBLISHING GROUP

We Chose Life
Why You Should Too

By Anthony Horvath

ATHANATOS
PUBLISHING GROUP

Published by the Athanatos Publishing Group
www.athanatosministries.org/group

Official Web Page of
We Chose Life: *Why You Should Too:*
www.wechoselife.com

There are study guides for this book available at the official web page.

Cover Design by Luke Thompson
www.sojournerdesign.org

About the Cover: The front cover is based on the picture of the actual room where the 'question' discussed in this book was asked.

ISBN 978-09822776-1-4

Printed in the United States of America

About the Author

Anthony Horvath is married and the father of four. His youngest daughter was born with Spina Bifida in 2007. In the course of discovering his daughter's condition he and his wife were asked if they wanted to 'terminate.' This book explains why they said "No!"

Anthony is a former teacher and is the author of a variety of fiction and non-fiction books. His columns have been published on several well known online news and commentary sites. He devotes much of his time to answering questions about why he believes that Christianity is true.

Anthony is available to speak with individuals who want to learn more or want to share their experiences. Or, if you are in a similar situation and don't know what to do, he is open to a phone call. He is also available to speak at churches, schools, and groups about his experiences. See the web site for contact information.

Table of Contents

Note: There are accompanying study guides available for this book, available for free on the webpage: www.wechoselife.com

Foreword

You probably have this book in your hands because you have just received terrible news: something is wrong with your baby. If that is the case, I can guess how you might be feeling. I know, because I've felt the same way. My wife and I found out at the 20 week ultrasound that our baby was a girl (that was good news!) with a severe birth defect called Spina Bifida. We were thrust into shock and remained there for a solid month. This period can really be described as a grieving period. I think you know what I mean.

The purpose of this book is to provide a measure of encouragement. Even grief is more bearable when we know that we are not alone in it. There are hundreds of thousands of people who have experienced what you and I have/are going through. We are not alone.

The book has another purpose, too. In many countries today, when parents are told that their child has a birth defect, the next question is "Do you want to terminate?" We were asked this question. We said "No!" If you are facing the same question we want you to know some of our reasons for choosing life.

It is entirely possible that you don't have to be persuaded to keep your child. That doesn't mean that you aren't riding an emotional roller coaster. I hope that you will still be helped by hearing our story. If, however, you are thinking about terminating your child, I hope that you will hear me out. After all: What is the rush? This is a short book. You can finish it in a sitting or two. This is the kind of decision that you'll want to think through. Don't let anyone push you into something.

Come along with me as I tell you my story.

My Story

My wife and I have four children through three pregnancies. Confused? So were we at the 20 week ultrasound of our second pregnancy. The ultrasound technician asked all sorts of odd questions prompting me to wonder if something was wrong and prompting my wife to wonder if perhaps she was further along than we had been led to believe. The technician snapped an image of what appeared to be two grape fruits in my wife's belly. It took a moment for reality to sink in: we were expecting twins. Twin boys.

It didn't take too long after that to realize that twins were going to be the death of us! They were three times the work of a single child. Because we already had a son, the birth of the twins meant that we were instantly out-numbered. One just had to get used to the fact that one child would always be unhappy... and screaming mad.

You can understand, then, why three years later we were looking forward to the next 20 week ultrasound with a special kind of eagerness. Yes, with three boys already, we very much wanted to see if our next child would be a girl. What reduced us to being nervous wrecks was the possibility that it would be twins again! We had to take the chance, though, since we knew that we wanted a girl before calling it 'quits.'

The day for the ultrasound of our third pregnancy was a pleasant December morning in 2006. We took our oldest son with us and enjoyed watching his reaction to the images on the monitor. We had two important questions for the ultrasound technician. First of all, were we looking at a girl? Secondly, was there only one girl?

With exuberant anticipation we explained to our son what he was seeing on the monitor while the technician did his work. The technician was surprisingly quiet. Neither of us thought much about it at the time, but we did notice it. We overlooked it in our joy at the news: it was a girl and it wasn't twins! Oddly, even after I jokingly asked him to check again, he only quietly repeated his assurance. In retrospect, his mood was easily understood. We would have much more important things to consider very shortly.

After the ultrasound, we went into one of the waiting rooms and chatted blissfully. We were ecstatic about the news and our enthusiasm washed over our son. I would have lit up a cigar right there if I had had one.

After just a few minutes, the doctor came

in. She wasn't smiling. Her expression was grim. There wasn't much time for us to adjust to this new tone. She went right to the point. Our new baby girl had a lot of fluid in her skull, a condition called hydrocephalus. The doctor told us that it could be just hydrocephalus, or, worst case scenario, it could mean that she had Spina Bifida. However, the opening in the spine could not be detected. My wife and I sat stunned. Our son continued his mirthful chattering completely unaware that the tides had changed and oblivious to the fact that we were all ignoring him.

We had heard of Spina Bifida but, like many people, didn't have a clue of what that condition really meant. We didn't understand how the hydrocephalus was related to the spinal defect. We had some familiarity with the condition because we knew of a child at church who had it but we were extremely fuzzy on the details.

That office was not the appropriate place to bone up on the details, either. The doctor told us there were mild cases as well as severe ones but before anything else, it was necessary to get another more detailed ultrasound. To my surprise, and our sincere gratitude, the doctor arranged for us to go to the hospital that very afternoon, in just a matter of a couple of hours, to see the doctor who specialized in such matters and get the confirmation we were looking for. We have since learned of couples who had to wait days for the next level ultrasound. It was so much better to find out quickly.

When we went home, my wife called her place of work and told them she wouldn't be able to come back that day. Thankfully, everyone was very understanding. Then we had to arrange for childcare for our three sons in the middle of the workday with no notice. What could have been a logistical nightmare resolved itself nicely. Our sitter was unexpectedly home and available rather than at work where we expected her to be.

While all these preparations were being made, I learned everything that I could about Spina Bifida by searching the Internet. It didn't look good.

Here is a summary of what I learned.

Spina Bifida is a condition in which an opening appears on the spine during the first few weeks of the baby's development. This opening is referred to as the 'defect.' The lower on the back the opening appears, the less function is affected. The spinal cord actually slips out of the opening. If you're lucky, it is contained in a sack of skin and fluids. Sometimes it is completely exposed.

Besides losing perhaps all sensation and movement in the legs and feet, it is very normal for Spina Bifida children to have problems with their bladders. Many of them will have to be catheterized several times a day until they get old enough to do it themselves. If you're wondering where the 'water on the brain' comes in, you're like me. How does a defect on the spine cause hydrocephalus?

Hydrocephalus is associated with other birth defects as well and can be a problem in its own right. Spina Bifida children frequently have hydrocephalus because when the spinal cord slips out of the opening in the bottom of the spine; this pulls the spinal cord down slightly, blocking the place in the back of the skull where the cerebrospinal fluid would normally drain. Our bodies are constantly creating and eliminating this fluid. Since the fluid can't escape, in a Spina Bifida child, it accumulates. Pressure gets placed on the brain which in turn puts pressure on the skull, making the head bigger than it normally would be. If the pressure is not relieved, there is brain damage.

A Spina Bifida child will usually have two

surgeries right off the bat. One is to deal with the opening on the spine and the other is to deal with the hydrocephalus, which usually entails putting in a shunt. The shunt is installed by drilling a hole in the skull and running a tube from the head, down the neck, and into the belly, or some other place where the cerebrospinal fluid can be disposed of by the body. The shunt has the potential for many future complications. It can become infected or blocked. The increased pressure in the brain can cause brain damage. If the shunt has to be modified, this can cause brain damage, also.

Though Spina Bifida is a defect of the spine, it typically affects almost every other part of the body. Naturally, every case is different. Some cases are worse than others.

As one might imagine, the uncertainty, coupled with our meager general knowledge of Spina Bifida, worked to create in our minds all of the worst case scenarios. I replayed them endlessly on the trip to the hospital, where we waited in the obstetrics lobby, our emotions taut and brittle. The 'best case' scenarios were as far from my mind as they could possibly be.

I have always lived by a simple principle: don't worry about things I can't control. Sometimes, the urgency of the moment compels itself and it is hard to live by that principle. The peace that comes from being content with one's limitations vanishes. This was such a moment. I was on the verge of panicking about things I could not control.

We were ushered back to see the doctor. He was cordial, though I wouldn't say warm. I didn't mind. At this point, we needed facts more than comfort. It didn't take long to get them, though it felt like an eternity at the time.

In the first ultrasound, the defect on the spine couldn't be spotted. Her condition was noticed because of the distinctive shape that her skull had and the fact that the ultrasound detected no brain: all it could see was cerebrospinal fluid. Finding the defect in this more thorough ultrasound would be critical in determining the next course of action.

The session was almost over and we still hadn't found the defect. At the last moment, she decided to do a complete flip within the womb, exposing her back to the doctor's ultrasound wand! There it was: the defect was discovered. Some tests would need to be run, but by appearances it was *myelomeningocele* spina bifida, which I had already learned in my rushed research was the most severe form of Spina Bifida.

I was surprised once again at how fast doctors can move when they so desire. This doctor advised amniocentesis which would find the tell-tale signs of an 'open defect.' He performed the procedure within five minutes, right there in the room. The amniotic fluid was sent away for testing and we were informed that we could have some preliminary information within a day or so. Now came the time for discussion.

We knew the 'question' was coming. I didn't know which doctor would be the one to pose it, but because of the doctor's no-nonsense demeanor I should have guessed that it would have been him.

"Will we keep this baby?"

(I believe his language was less sentimental, but I don't recall specifically now. It was all a haze to us. My wife remembers details I don't, and I remember details she doesn't).

I had already decided in my mind that we would, we absolutely would keep this child, and I knew that my wife had already made the same decision. We had made the decision years before. The time to make such decisions is well in advance of 'the moment.' Still, I felt that I should let my wife speak for herself. I thought it would be more significant if the doctor heard it from her and not me. Though the whole morning had been filled with tension and uncertainty, I will remember with pride to the day that I die what my wife said:

"There is no question of us keeping this baby."

For the record, we didn't think that the doctor was trying to push us in any direction. There was some hint to the effect that the child would have lots of health issues that would be quite severe and these would affect our lives, but it wasn't pressed. He didn't try to talk us out of the decision but went quickly on to discussing those next steps. I am aware of doctors who would have continued to press the point so I want to give this doctor the credit due him.

The next step was meeting with the genetic counselor at the hospital. In retrospect, we really should have waited until the test results were back because he didn't have much to say and we caught him on his way to another appointment. We ended up coming back a few days later when test results were in hand and it was a more productive meeting. After the initial sit-down, it was time for the ride home.

I cannot put into words the cloud that was over us.

What had we learned?

We learned that there was definitely severe

swelling within the baby's head and that it was pretty certain that her Spina Bifida was the worst case 'open defect' type. In a moment of rationality we were able to remind ourselves that, even in our brief researches, these 'worst cases' would have outcomes spanning a wide spectrum. Yes, it could be a 'worst case' scenario. Or it might not be. Yes, it could be that she was severely mentally handicapped, that she would have to be catheterized her entire life, that she would not walk, that she would be confined to a wheel chair... that she could succumb... But she may not end up with any of these things. Here was the brutal reality: there was no way of knowing the future.

There were numerous variables. For example, we would only know about her mental abilities after the shunt was inserted to drain off the excess fluid in her head. If you get it early enough, before the skull 'hardens,' the prospects are generally good. Nonetheless, there was no way of knowing for sure until that moment: 20 weeks later. There was also no way of knowing what kind of sensation and movement she would have below the waist. We were told that we probably wouldn't know this until she was a year or more old.

As we drove home in silence, I descended into the depths of self-pity. I had thoughts, some of which I will not dare to share here. Of some, I am merely embarrassed. Of others, I am ashamed. *Kyrie Eleison.*[1] Together, my wife and I entered the grieving process although no one had actually died.

But that isn't really true. Someone did die. When we first envisioned having a daughter we had pictures in our head of what that would be like. There were the normal images, of course: her first steps, her first birthday, crawling, scaling steps. Then there were images of cute dresses, a little girl out collecting flowers, playing catch, and more like these... then others, like the Homecoming Dance, and Prom night... and a wedding, where father and daughter dance one last significant dance. The girl in all these images was dead. She would not be.

We mourned the daughter we would not have.

In the midst of these dark thoughts there were the practical questions. How would we explain this to friends? What about our family? What about our three sons? How would we explain this to our oldest son, who

---

[1] Latin for "Lord, Have Mercy." See associated study guide for discussion.

just hours ago was overflowing with joy?

I ended up not calling my folks, who live out of state, until a day or two later. As every one was interested in hearing the results (was it twins? If so, twin boys? Again??!?), I suspected that possibly my mother and father were hurt not to have heard from us that day. I could not bring myself to tell friends that day, the next day, or the day after. I don't know when I told them, actually. Perhaps it was a full week. I suspect our silence was noticed. It seemed prudent to wait until we had the results back from the amniocentesis, even though we did have some very concrete indications in hand.

Explaining the matter to parents and grandparents was difficult. Everyone had heard of Spina Bifida but like us, no one really knew what it was. In our grief, we had to explain what it was and what the implications were. It was bad enough that we couldn't just blurt out the problem - we had to flesh out the whole thing, the very last thing we wanted to do.

It was a very awkward period for my wife and me. A time of joy had been dashed. I had just published a book a week or so before the ultrasound and had planned on a full scale Christmas marketing campaign for it. This, too, was dashed. Only two weeks later, we went to my folks (out of state) for Christmas and, as expected, found family as uncomfortable to talk about the matter as we were. Perhaps it would have been better to just get it all out in the open. By this time, all the test results were in and the diagnosis made. Everything was upside down.

Something happened after that first full first week, though. We passed through our despair and entered forcefully into resolve. Fine, the daughter we had expected would not be, but there was going to be a daughter, nonetheless. We were going to love this child.

And that thought ends the other thoughts.

We stood up under the crushing reality and decided we were not going to be slaves to it.

By this time, the prayers of God's people had begun in earnest. Friends and family were praying, 'strangers' from the Internet were praying, friends of friends were praying. One always wonders if people who say they are praying actually do pray. I know that is a problem I have always struggled with myself. For quite a few years now I have been of the mind that I won't even say I will pray for someone unless I know quite well that I will. But in this case, it was clear, abundantly clear, that there were intercessions on our behalf.

God answered those prayers initially in the strength of our resolve and our reconciliation with our lost dreams and expectations. There would be other evidences to come. One of the continuing difficulties of our situation was that we were stuck in this limbo where we knew that things did not look good but we could not be sure whether they were very bad or not. We had to gratefully decline offers of assistance as we couldn't even know if we needed it.

We chose not to tell our oldest son until much later in the pregnancy. For one thing, he couldn't be trusted not to tell everyone and their mother about it. During the months of February and March, although we were increasingly more comfortable talking about the situation, we didn't like the idea of fielding sincere inquiries about the baby based on an unknown reality. We always gave people the wide spectrum of outcomes and left it at that. That was an awkward place to leave things, so we preferred not even to 'go there.'

The time went slowly. We had to make efforts to ensure that there were ultrasounds to monitor the baby's development, but there was pretty much nothing for us to do except wait for the big day. A few things we knew. We knew, for example, that on the 'big day,' she would be delivered by c-section. We knew that our neurosurgeon would first close the defect in the back. He would wait a day or two and then have the head and brain surgery whereby the shunt would be implanted. She was due on May 13th, 2007. A c-section date of May 8th was set, with the back surgery to follow on the 9th.

Oh how little we know!

On April 16th, my wife and I went into the clinic to view the c-section video. The previous two pregnancies were 'natural' births so the information on c-sections was appreciated. I dare say my wife was getting pretty large by now!

The video reminded us of our trepidation. Just the week before, we went in to see the ultrasound doctor again and he was concerned by some of the things that he saw. Quote: "When your baby is born, she is going to be a very sick baby." When we pressed for more information he said that she'd have many complications and implied that there might be brain and/or organ damage. One thing that did please him was the baby's size. She was doing quite well on that front and my wife bore the evidence of that!

The next day, on April 17th, I was working outside on the house. My wife had reported not feeling well but there wasn't much we could do about it. I did my thing and chatted with the neighbors. Shortly after talking with a neighbor about the prospects of the baby coming early, my wife stuck her head out of the door and explained, in more crystal clear terms, that she was not comfortable. There was some confusion as to whether or not her water had broken. Finally, we determined that it would be prudent to head to the hospital, which we did immediately.

Within the hour we were at the hospital and shortly after that it was determined that, in fact, her water had broken. There was some confusion, at least in my mind, but eventually I did get from a doctor a clear "Yes, her water did break." They were talking about having the c-section but that point was ambiguous to us. My guess is that they had all communicated it to each other and assumed someone had communicated it to us. Not a big deal.

The preparations began. The nurses and doctors all knew that our daughter had Spina Bifida but I reminded them anyway that such children were often allergic to latex. Now the first curve ball came: The doctor that would be delivering the baby informed us that our neurosurgeon was out of town and could not perform the operations.

Naturally, we inquired into which neurosurgeon would be given the task. We were informed that the neurosurgeon on call did not think it appropriate to perform the operations because the matter was best handled by a pediatric neurosurgeon and he was not one.

You can probably guess how exasperated I felt as I guessed that their statements were leading to some conclusion. "Alright, just who would be doing the surgery?" I wanted to know. The answer: the baby would be immediately air-lifted to a university hospital system where a pediatric neurosurgeon would perform the surgeries. It would take just a half an hour or so for our daughter to arrive at the university hospital, but this new wrinkle meant that one of us would have a two and a half hour drive the next day. Since I wasn't going to be the one giving birth, you can guess who that person would be.

Once again, numerous logistical problems were miraculously resolved even before our daughter was born. Childcare was established since I wouldn't be able to provide it and arrangements were set in motion to bring my wife over to the university hospital as quickly as possible.

Around 9 p.m., my wife was rolled in for

the surgery. I had made the necessary calls to get things rolling, including passing along some prayer requests. I was scrubbed in but would be escorted into the operating room only after they had come reasonably close to delivering. I paced the hospital room like a trapped lion. We were now very close to the moment of truth, and I was helpless in determining the outcome. Our daughter had not yet received her name. We had narrowed our choices down to two names. One meant 'noble.' The other meant 'reborn.' We would wait and see how she was before assigning the name. In light of my discussion about possible outcomes, I'll leave the reader to ponder why we might assign one and not the other.

I was bordering on frantic when they escorted my wife into the operating room. After just a few moments, they invited me to peer over the veil to see our daughter emerge from my wife's belly. I declined the offer to 'cut the cord.' I'd had about enough of that! Besides, I was more interested in the fact that our daughter wasn't making any noise. I watched anxiously as the nurses tried to clean her up and get her breathing. It seemed like there was some success but we couldn't be sure. She was rushed to the NICU and they urgently waved me to follow. I watched as they continued to clean her up. At last she was breathing and, bless her, crying. There were hordes of doctors and nurses around her, making it difficult to get a look at her. When I did, I watched her legs and her feet for movement. I noted the size of the defect. I observed how big her head was - or wasn't. We were told that this baby would be born very sick, and indeed there had been indications up to the last week that this would be so. I saw indications to the contrary.

The name was chosen: Reborn.

Her head was slightly swollen but not nearly to the extent I feared as I had looked at the ultrasounds. In the ultrasounds, there was so much 'water' that we could not even see her brain. I was cautiously optimistic about her smaller than expected head size. The defect was present - it was definitely myelomeningocele - but compared to some pictures I had seen online it was not overly huge, and it was low in the back, the best place you could have such a defect occur. I saw two legs moving. I thought I saw a foot moving.

Yes, her name is *Reborn*.

That is what her full name *means*. We will call her, for short, Renny, for the rest of the story.

There wasn't much time to do a thorough

review because they were prepping her for the move to the university hospital just as soon as they could. In fact, the helicopter crew seemed to be so impatient to get moving that I feared that my wife would not be allowed to see her baby before she was air-lifted. I was assured that this would not happen but then another doctor or nurse would come in and I would wonder. I suppose it is unlikely that anyone would have dared to whisk a stable child out without being seen by her mother but there was very little for me to do. So what few tasks I had left, I aimed to do well. Protecting the interests of my family was high on my list. Long story short, they did bring her in for my wife to see. In retrospect, unlikely or not, I think they would have taken her away if I hadn't kept reminding the new doctors in the room that my wife hadn't yet seen the baby.

It wasn't long after my wife saw Renny that the helicopter took off. I videotaped its going with a dull weight in my stomach. Everything was upside down. Once again, all expectations had been dashed. Who knew what the morrow would bring?

I slept at the hospital that night and in the morning went home to get affairs in order. I had wanted to leave in time to be at the hospital before the surgeries began, which I expected would be in the early afternoon. However, we received a phone call that the surgery was expected to begin as early as 10 or 11 a.m. As there was no way I could make that, I focused on getting everything in order.

We also learned that the neurosurgeon at the university hospital had a different way of doing things than our local neurosurgeon. Instead of doing the surgeries separately, he would do them together, during the same operation. The back would be closed up and then the shunt would be installed. Allegedly this cut down on the risk of infection. Sure, whatever. It wasn't like I had time to look into it, now!

Incidentally, the change in neurosurgeons greatly complicated matters for months to come. We had to choose between the two doctors. Ultimately, the local one was 'let go' from our hospital, leaving us to wonder how 'fortunate' we were to have had our daughter while he was on vacation.

Anyway, I finally got on the road around 1 p.m.. I made some additional phone calls to people that I had left hanging but otherwise drove at a normal speed though I had really wanted to drive ninety miles an hour. A phone call from my wife informed me that in fact the operation didn't even start until early afternoon. Another call from her informed me that I needed to call the neurosurgeon ASAP, as he wanted to do an entirely different procedure than the one that we had anticipated. Everything upside down! Instead of a shunt, the doctor wanted to do something else called an ETV. If conditions were not right for the ETV, they would simply install the shunt. The same place in the skull is opened in either case. I learned later that 'conditions being right' meant avoiding hitting a vein that would almost certainly result in death, if nicked.

But I learned that later.

Here I was, not even on the site, being asked to consider a procedure that I knew absolutely nothing about except whatever the doctor shared with me in our brief exchange. I had put in some effort into being as informed as I could about my daughter's condition and some of the treatments but this was the first that I had heard of an ETV! (It turns out that this is because our local neurosurgeon thought it a bad idea.)

I wasn't very happy about being put on the spot but I was informed that Renny was on the table and a decision had to be made. The neurosurgeon emphatically stated that if it

22

were his daughter, this is what he would do. The arguments for it did seem valid. There are a lot of health issues that arise on account of a shunt and if the cerebrospinal fluid could be drained without one, then that was a good idea. I did what I could: I made the decision and then quickly called a friend. I asked him to alert some other friends whom I knew would be praying for us and would pray for us and told him the situation. After that, it was out of my control, and I ceased fretting about it.

Ironically, after all that stress, it was determined that the ETV procedure could not be done. Instead, they installed the traditional shunt. Was this Providence? In light of the potential risk with the ETV necessitating special care to miss the vital vein, was the doctor guided by God, acting on the prayers of others, to recognize that the procedure could not be done safely? I suppose we will not know for sure this side of the veil, but I know what I believe.

Finally I got to see our precious daughter beyond a passing glance. I was pleased to see that she was still moving her legs and at least one foot. She would be seen moving her other foot the next day. It was not full mobility, but the prospects were good. It was unnerving to see the big bulge on her scalp where the shunt had been put in but, like I said, we were going to love this child, come hell or high water.

I stayed that first night at the hospital but the next evening drove home to pick my wife up from the hospital.

Amazingly, though born three to four weeks early, she was a good size: 7 pounds 5 ounces. Our twin boys had been 6-1 and 7-4, so she was even bigger than two of our other children. She had no breathing complications. Apart from just having spine and brain surgeries, she was one of the healthiest babies in the NICU!

On Sunday, after only 5 days, we came home. Long before, we had been led to expect that she was going to be in the hospital for nearly 14 days. This was in part because the previous neurosurgeon was going to do the two surgeries on different days. Now nearly three hours from home, we would have been quite dismayed if we would have had to be away from home for so long. Everything was upside down, but it could have been worse.

Today, it must be confessed that things still are pretty upside down. They are 'upside down' in some good ways, too. For example, unlike many other Spina Bifida children who need to be catheterized frequently, except for a brief period in the beginning, we have not had to catheterize our daughter. Her bladder empties on its own. She sometimes is constipated, but in general her bowels empty on their own, too. You can imagine how this makes our lives considerably easier but more importantly what that will mean to her dignity as she gets older: providing she retains this function. A lot can change because of infections and other complications. For now, though, this change of expectations is a change for the better.

Her legs and feet still show motion, although a little less than what she showed those first few days. Still, her back healed nicely and her shunt has not been infected even once. As this is being written, she is in a full body cast because of hip surgery (both her hips are dislocated). Nonetheless, the prospects are good that one day she will, in fact, be able to walk. As for her intellect, she was born slightly prematurely which is a factor, but all in all, she seems as bright and adorable as can be. She makes everyone feel happy. Renny makes everyone feel special. Even in her body cast she pulls herself across the room, exploring nooks and crannies. She is almost as far away from the 'worst possible outcome' as you can get. We would have loved her anyway, but we are thankful, especially for her sake, that things have been good for her.

This is our story, from grief to hope. Throughout the experience there have been moments of crisis that 'miraculously' resolved themselves. As difficult as things were (and are) we have never found them to be impossible. Not only that, our daughter has brought a joy into our lives that we didn't have before. Her victories are more monumental than the ones our sons experienced, because she has to fight against the odds to achieve them.

All in all, you might say that our story ended quite well (though it must be added that a lot can change and the tale is still young). You might be right. There can be no doubt that many people have had children with far worse outcomes, including many Spina Bifida children. This really is the point, though. One doesn't know how the story might end. One can't know. For all you know, it might end well. It might even end better than our story! Since you don't know, doesn't it seem prudent not to worry about the things you can't control and pray and hope for the best?

Why We Kept Our Baby

The abortion debate is complicated and multi-faceted. I wouldn't dare think that I could give an exhaustive treatment of every aspect of it in this short little book. Nor will I spend a lot of time developing what I do put in here. I expect that a lot of readers will be people who are suddenly faced with a similar situation, have recently emerged from a difficult decision, or perhaps simply have found themselves with an unexpected, but healthy, pregnancy. One of my chief contentions is that the best time to address the matter is long before you are in the situation where you have to decide. For this reason, in this book I will raise questions to think about and offer answers that make sense to me. It doesn't mean that these are the only questions or the only answers, or even the best questions or answers. I hope that with these caveats in mind you will listen to what I have to share.

You Just Don't Know

In the late 1990s a baby was born alive at Christ Hospital in Oak Lawn, Illinois. This was an accident: the intention had been to abort the child but it survived the abortion procedure. According to Jill Stanek, the nurse who blew the whistle on such activities, the baby had been aborted because it had Spina Bifida. Only it didn't have Spina Bifida. It had been a mistaken diagnosis. This baby boy was taken into a utility room to die. Later, the father came and saw what had happened, and walked out of the room without saying a word. I wonder what he was thinking.

Every birth defect is different, so the level of certainty about potential outcomes is different, too. However, generally speaking, there are mild and severe forms of every condition. It doesn't matter if we are talking about Cerebral Palsy, Down Syndrome, or Spina Bifida. To consider your decision as though the worst case scenario is inevitable just isn't very reasonable.

I do not mean to imply that if you had absolute certainty that the worst case scenario was going to play out that you should then terminate your child. As my opening story illustrates, you can never be certain if only because doctors can make mistakes. Let me tell you some other reasons.

In the first place, the idea of 'absolute certainty' must be measured against the fact that medical science continues to press forward, often making great strides in a short time. The outcome that seems absolutely certain today might be doubtful tomorrow. What if they discover how to use adult stem cells to re-create nerve endings, for example? What if they figure out how to modify the genome itself in a living, breathing, human (gene therapy)? In other words, what if the cure for whatever condition you're encountering right now *is actually found* a year or so from now?

Let me be clear about my argument, here. I am not trying to instill a wishful hope in your mind. You shouldn't make this decision because you expect or hope for a positive outcome, either. My concern is that the 'worst case scenario' is given over-riding emphasis when we think about this issue. Trust me, I know. When we were told that our daughter had Spina Bifida the only outcomes I contemplated were the bad ones. Even when I reminded myself that there were positive outcomes, too, I still had trouble fighting back the impulse to dwell on the worst possible scenarios.

Yes, it might turn out that it is the 'worst case scenario' and things might be very difficult for you for the rest of your life. That is true, but you can't base your decision on that because for all you know, it might end up being the 'best case scenario.' Even more, they might find a cure altogether!

With that said, even in so-called 'worst case scenarios' the children can still bring you immense joy. I know of several such cases and the parents love their child a great deal. Much depends on attitude.

As hard as it is to ponder life with a special needs child imagine a life where you 'terminated' your child only to find out it had been a mistake. Imagine a life where a short time after you 'terminated' your child the cure for your child's condition was found, or barring that, perhaps an astounding leap in medical science is discovered that dramatically alleviates the condition. *You just don't know.*

Doctors Can Be Wrong

Speaking of medical science, if you will recall from our story, in one of ultrasounds just prior to having Renny the doctor announced to us that our daughter would be born with 'lots of problems.' And by all appearances, the doctor was right. There seemed to be anomalies in the internal organs and there were other concerns. In the end, apart from more 'run of the mill' circumstances related to Spina Bifida, she had-

and has continued to have- very few problems related to these 'anomalies.'

Was this because of Divine Intervention, as I tend to think, or was it simply because the doctor was wrong? Do you see that it doesn't make a difference? The outcome was not as predicted!

Remember the story from earlier as recounted by Jill Stanek on pages 27-28? The child was 'terminated' because it was thought he would have Spina Bifida. When the baby was born it was learned that there had been a mistake. *The doctors had been wrong.*

For reasons already given, even if the doctors are right that doesn't justify aborting a living person who is innocent in every way. However, the raw fact is that doctors can be wrong, and often are. At my local hospital, there are signs posted everywhere that say: "Check every time: Right Patient? Right Procedure? Right Location?" Why? Because the best of us can make mistakes. Even with the best information in hand, the best information can lead the best trained people to wrong conclusions.

Abortion is already hard to live with. Imagine living with it having found out that you 'terminated' a perfectly healthy child.

The arguments to this point rest to a

degree on a certain assumption. Namely, I am assuming that we agree that we are talking about a thing worth preserving, a child, an honest to goodness human child. What if you don't share that assumption with me?

The Unborn are Due the Rights and Privileges We Extend to all Persons

Let us first clarify an important point. No one disputes that life begins at conception any more. As far as being a separate, living entity, the new embryo is most certainly that. But is it *human* life? And even if it is *human* life, does that mean that 'personhood' begins at conception? It is on these two latter points that there is dispute.

Is it a human life? In some circles, people loathe calling it a human life. Saying something is human automatically implies 'personhood.' Clearly, though, this life is human, even if it is in a different stage of development. No one disputes that the embryo resulting from an eagle is an eagle embryo. Likewise, the embryo resulting from a human is a human embryo. Though there are some that dispute this there aren't many. Allow me to focus on what I think is the real crux of the issue- personhood.

Here we need to ask ourselves whether or not there are significant differences as far as 'personhood' goes in different stages of development. For example, if we point to a human in the stage of 'adolescence,' i.e., human adolescence, are they any less a person? If they are a person while in the stage of human adolescence why aren't they in the stage of human embryo?

For example, consider the views of Peter Singer, a bioethicist and atheistic secular humanist, who said: "Simply killing an infant is never equivalent to killing *a person*." (NY Times, 1999. Emphasis mine.)

You get the idea.

We begin to be able to sharpen the issue to the true underlying question: "If an embryo is not a person all along, when *exactly* does it become one?" The assumption is that if it is a person, it is entitled to the rights and privileges we extend to persons.

A pro-life person would not merely assert that life begins at conception, but that personhood does, as well. The pro-choice side cannot be as unambiguous. Let us consider why.

What we are looking for is some non-arbitrary point at which we can finally say "Aha! Now the embryo is a person!"

There are various attempts to establish criteria. For example, for a long time it was maintained that once a fetus was viable, we could treat it as a person. Another questionable criterion is the belief that there can't be a person without personality, and you can't have a personality without a thinking brain. Proponents of this view might make brainwave activity the measure of the question.

There are some people who are positively indifferent. But for many of us, it is not so easy to dismiss the question. So, assuming the personhood of the embryo would decide the question, what advantages are there to criteria such as viability or brainwave activity? The chief advantage is that under these conditions, the embryo more closely resembles 'persons' as we are used to seeing them. However, there are some fundamental flaws to such criteria.

In the first place, these measures are not very measurable! Nor are they always the same in every pregnancy. With the advances in technology we know that what is not viable today might be viable tomorrow, and really the only way one could find out is if one tried it giving birth to an embryo only a few months old. There may come a point (if it hasn't already been reached) when technology and expertise exists to allow an embryo to be 'viable' from conception! What happens to the argument then?

The real conundrum remains as to whether or not we would ever be able to put our finger on any precise place where 'personhood' definitely is there.

Secondly, we need consistent definitions of 'personhood' that can be reasonably applied to other situations. What about the famous comatose person kept alive only because of technology? Does a person in a car accident cease to be a person because for a short time he is not 'viable'? What about the people who wake up from their comas years, even decades later? Were they not persons in the meantime? (What if most comatose people actually came out of their comas if we only waited long enough?)

There is no question that defining death can be a tricky matter but note this important distinction: at least with death we presume personhood and make every effort to revive someone if at all possible. If we really believed they weren't persons in the meantime, it is hard to see why anyone but the loved ones would care.

Now, if we aren't willing to apply the logic consistently throughout all stages of human experience, we need to ask ourselves how we are going to justify it just in one case: the unborn human.

Against this let me set this absolutely true statement: Apart from birth itself, the only objective, non-arbitrary point in human development that can be defined with near pinpoint accuracy is the moment of conception.

There isn't anything else.

My argument is simply this: if in the case of the dead and dying we presume personhood and bend over backwards to revive and preserve the person, shouldn't we extend the same courtesy to the unborn, who haven't even the ability to craft a do-not-resuscitate order - or the ability to defend themselves in any way?

Who Decides on Personhood?

Who exactly has the right to decide precisely when an entity gains or loses their status as a person? Let me submit this sobering thought: if brilliant humans throughout history haven't been able to nail it down is it wise to take the chance that what you're 'terminating' isn't actually a person? Are you so certain it is worth the chance?

Here is a fundamental question: "Precisely *who* decides when a person is a person?"

There are two basic answers to our question. Either humans themselves decide when personhood begins and ends, or something other than humans do.

It is really as simple as that.

If we say that humans decide, then we are faced with the uneasy truth that humans can change their minds and can make 'wrong' decisions. History is filled with exactly this. The Germans decided that the Jews were not 'persons'. The massacre of the residents of the tiny hamlet of My Lai, in Vietnam, was perpetuated by soldiers who had decided that the Vietnamese were not 'persons.' There is little we can say to condemn them, at least on rational grounds, if humans are the final arbiters of 'personhood.' Who are we to tell one human what a person is if the matter is decided by humans? It would be our private opinion about 'persons' against theirs. In the same way, we have no basis for decrying Peter Singer's views that infants are not automatically persons.

The other side of the coin is very uncomfortable for some people. If it isn't humans that decide, what does that leave?

The obvious contender is God.

If you believe that there is a God then you probably understand that He is the one that makes the call. If the unborn are persons, it is because He makes them persons, and our opinion on the matter hardly matters. Do you believe in God? Do you believe in a God that values persons? If so, the conclusion here is clear.

If not, this is a question you need to come to terms with because I have already explained what the consequences are for this question if you believe that 'personhood' is decided by humans alone. I am banking on the fact that you have a heart and are repulsed by the Holocaust and the My Lai massacre. How does one escape the implications inherent in allowing humans to decide when a human is a person? In the examples I gave, the depersonalization involved has been extensively documented. Can one retain humans as the ultimate authority on personhood and still condemn atrocities done by humans?

You can see why it is important to think through these matters before you're actually in a situation where you must act. It is hard enough if you have to consider what to do with the knowledge that your child has some debilitating condition. Do you now have to decide on the question of God, too?

This is not the place for a long discussion on why you should believe in God. I would submit that the fact that nearly everyone is repulsed by human atrocities seems to suggest that we all share a common moral code, which suggests the existence of an objective morality. I ask this simple question again: *"What if you're wrong?"*

What if *You're* Wrong?

What I am describing here may sound an awful lot like Pascal's Wager. Blaise Pascal meant it differently than it is often presented today. In his argument, one had to make the decision based on equal evidence in both directions. So, if you had evidence for the existence of God and evidence against the existence of God, and they were perfectly equal, you'd choose belief in God because the rewards were exceptional - if you were right. If you were wrong, however, you lost nothing. You simply became dirt. That was basically his argument, though as I said, it has become distorted.[2]

It is not my purpose to offer Pascal's

---

[2] This is discussed more in the associated study guide. Pascal's Wager is introduced in his *Pensées* as a culmination of a long discussion on the merits of Christianity.

Wager as an argument for why you should believe in God. Instead I want to present it in the context of our discussion about the unborn.

In Pascal's Wager the only person involved is the one making the choice. Only the one weighing the evidence is being prompted to choose the option with the most rewards. In our context, though, there is at stake another person.

In other words, what if you are wrong about when life begins? How confident are you that the evidence supports one position over another? What is at stake is not an abstraction but, conceivably another, living human being.

Moreover, it is appropriate to apply this reasoning to the question of God's existence even in this context. Your conclusion about God potentially will affect the lives of those around you, including the life of the one inside the mother's womb. Are you so sure that there is no God that you are willing to take another life? Are you so sure that there is no God that you are certain that that life is not a 'person'?

I'm not asking you to believe in God, per se. I'm asking you to err on the side of caution. At the end of all things, you might just discover that there is a God, after all. You might just discover that the millions of unborn aborted around the world actually are persons, created by God. What then will you say? The evidence wasn't good enough? Do you think that will cut it?

Of course, it is logically possible that there isn't a God. So, what have you risked? You carried a baby to term. You had several months of discomfort and inconvenience. Whether you keep the child or abort you will be a changed person. If you keep the child and find that the situation is bigger than you can handle there is always the choice of adoption. Keeping the child leaves numerous options on the table, but aborting it leaves no options, and is irreversible.

What if you're wrong? The question is worth repeating in numerous contexts. How sure are you of your conclusions about reality? One thing we can be sure of: there is no going back if you abort.

The 'Wager' still applies. If you can't decisively state when personhood begins then it is prudent to err on the side of caution. If the evidence is equally dubious to you on both sides then shouldn't the 'default' position be that we preserve life?

This is precisely how we handle the matter from the other side, when we are trying to figure out when life and personhood ends. We bend over backwards to preserve the rights of individuals when they are on their deathbed. Why wouldn't we do the same with the unborn?

Equal Under the Law

We might argue that even if we can't be sure that embryos are actually persons, that doesn't mean we can't treat them as though they were persons. Think of it this way: though we often talk about how we are all created equal, the truth is that we are actually all very different. There are people with different physical strengths, for example. There are people with different mental capacities. Nonetheless, we consider every person as equal under the law. In other words, we have established a fiction as far as the law goes. In this way, we are able to preserve the rights and dignity of everyone, no matter how different they might be.

This equality under the law was designed specifically out of fear that humans would decide the value of other humans. They were concerned that people might give special privileges to some and not others and that the people making the decision could also change their minds. One might hope that the people deciding the question were trustworthy, good, and decent. True, they might be benevolent; but they may not be. Just in case, the founders of our country determined that the rule of the land would be that we are all equal under the law.

There is nothing that prevents us from extending the same rights and privileges to the unborn as we do anyone else. The only noticeable difference is that the unborn are not in a position to protest if we don't. They should not be penalized for being defenseless.

As I have argued, we might all wake up one day and through some miracle discover without a doubt that we were wrong about everything. There is no God and 'personhood' is a fiction of our own making. (Of course, if atheism is true we do not actually ever discover this.) What would we have lost? Nothing much. After a relatively brief period of (potentially intense) discomfort you could allow the child to be adopted and wash your hands of the matter.

If, however, we discover that there is a God and that personhood is bestowed by God, then we will consider ourselves blessed that in the midst of our ignorance we did not do anything dire and irreversible.

Other Arguments

The above sums up the central thrust of my own views. You can guess that my wife and I had long decided that there was a God, that life is a gift of God, and that we have no business ending *innocent* life unless we have extremely compelling reasons (i.e., we might debate the death penalty or collateral damage in warfare). We do not believe that we have the right to de-classify something as a person just because to do otherwise means we will be inconvenienced. Also, we don't believe that a child is a 'punishment.' God isn't happy about the state of the world but he doesn't inflict bad things on people just to prove points. Moreover, if you read our story closely you will see places where we reasonably inferred that God was with us during the ordeal. In other words, He may seem absent but He is not absent.

There are other arguments that people have raised concerning such issues and I wanted to touch on some of them. I know that I cannot be exhaustive or comprehensively treat every objection. I can only give you a start and then it will be up to you to pick up the ball and run with it.

Potentiality

One reason why people argue that we should construe the unborn as a living, human, person is because there is no question that what starts out looking like a small mass of cells always becomes, indisputably, a living, human person. If the process is left to itself, 100% of the time, a baby emerges.

Some people take issue with the idea that a 'small mass of cells' should be treated as anything like a human. Of course, if you are reading this because you just received unfortunate news at your 20 week ultrasound then you know already that you aren't talking about a 'small mass of cells.' On the ultrasound you saw, unmistakably, a human. Still, prior to this appearance, people have issues treating the fetus or embryo like a person because it is no bigger at some stages than a bacterium or a tumor.

The counter to this is straight-forward common sense. If ever this 'small mass of cells' ever turned into something other than a human child, we could talk. If, for example, instead of a human baby a woman gave birth to a monkey, we would re-consider. If, instead, the woman sprouted a leg from her head instead of having a baby, we would recant the whole thing. There is absolutely no question (assuming nothing goes wrong, which is very different) that we are talking about something distinctly human which will be- if it isn't already- a human person.

As such, the embryo should be accorded the rights and privileges we accord all other persons.

The Life Destroyed

In some quarters it is argued that having the baby will destroy the life of the parents, or the mother in particular. There may be difficulties in affording the child. Perhaps the mother will have to suspend her career. Perhaps she will be reduced to poverty. For the good of the mother, and possibly the father, too, it is urged sometimes that 'termination' occur. This reasoning can be employed both in cases where the baby has been determined to be 'special needs' and also when the child is perfectly healthy.

Here I must again point out that you cannot possibly know for sure that it is going to work out all this way, and even if it did, it wouldn't follow that the child simply ceases to become a person, un-entitled to the rights and privileges of a person.

I know something about this, too. My mother had me when she was 16. Roe versus Wade had made abortion legal so she had a legal right to 'terminate' me if she had wanted to. Has my mother had a more difficult life than she would have had if she had 'terminated' me? Let me be plain: had she never conceived me her life would almost certainly have been much easier. She has had to work harder and her career opportunities have been limited. Does she regret having me? No.

Barack Obama's mother had him when she was only 18. Her life has been difficult, no doubt, but do you think she regrets it? No. Sarah Palin gave birth to a baby with Down Syndrome. This is a very complicated and involved condition which will put significant stress on her family. Does she regret having this child? No. Sarah Palin's own daughter, Bristol, is pregnant with a child at only the age of 17. Will Bristol have a more difficult life than she would have had? Absolutely. Will she have regrets? Yes. Will she regret having her child? No.

Why not? Because just as you can't possibly know that things will turn out badly you can't know that they won't turn out good, either. Though their lives are transformed, the

47

young mothers and fathers are not necessarily enslaved to the 'worst case scenario.' There are difficulties, but there are joys, too. For all one knows, the child will grow up to be someone remarkable. Even if that is not the case, the child can grow up loved, and when everything is said and done, life is only about the people in it. Careers fade away, money dwindles, to dust we return, but relationships are what give life value and meaning. Sometimes the 'unplanned' relationships are the most rewarding.

A disabled child can bring much joy into your life. Some say that the joy is even more amazing because there is so much less taken for granted. One assumes that their child will walk. But if your Spina Bifida child walks, that is a victory beyond victories.

It should be pointed out that it is an illusion to think that, having obtained an abortion, all will be well. Many women report intense guilt at having aborted their children. Many fall into depression. The decision to abort has disastrous effects on women (and others who are involved in an abortion decision). No matter how you approach it, once a woman becomes pregnant her life is never the same. Aborting the baby does not change this and in fact is known to create its own problems. So, if you can expect to have difficulties no matter which way you go (even birthing 'wanted' children means having difficulties) you may as well choose life.

But What About the Woman's Body?

In this objection, it is maintained that the living, breathing, human comes about only because it 'borrows' from the woman's 'resources.' And doesn't the woman have the right to decide where she 'spends' her 'resources'?

The problem with this objection is like many other objections. Where would the logic end?

A newborn baby is as dependent on the mother as it was inside the mother, just in a different way. If you do not feed it and take care of it, it will die. The only difference here is the 'resources' in question. Instead of the organic resources of blood, protein, nutrients, etc, the resources in question are more material: money for formula, diapers, etc.

The fact that the child is dependent doesn't affect their status as a person. If it is a person despite being 'dependent' outside the womb, there is no reason it isn't a person while in the womb, too.

The fact that the woman is forced to use some of her resources, albeit some very intimate ones, does not change the fact that the child is a person. If it is a person, then we are not permitted merely to think in terms of only the "woman's body."

If I could be assured with 100% certainty that the child absolutely was not a person by any measure then I would drop these objections. In fact, everything to this point would be moot. While I sympathize with the plight of women who find themselves in this situation unexpectedly, I cannot see how the imposition to her body justifies the death of a person, especially because after a short time the imposition is over, and she can then make plans for the child to be adopted if she prefers.

This last segment is probably irrelevant for many readers. They were probably hoping for a baby to begin with and the idea of sharing the mother's 'resources' was not the issue.

However, on the chance that a young woman finds herself unexpectedly pregnant and then finds this book in her hands, it seemed like I should make some comments about this particular objection. Similarly, I thought it would be relevant for those trying to form their opinions before the 'moment of decision' is upon them.

Conclusion

I don't know how this book got into your hands or in what situation you find yourself. You may have just had the world come crashing down on your shoulders. You might know someone personally who is in such a crisis. Perhaps you are just thinking through the issues in pursuit of the truth.

I can't possibly speak to everyone at the same time. I hope that some of my argumentation has been received in the spirit it is offered. That saying, 'It is easier said than done' is something I know is true, first hand. It is easier to say 'keep the child even though you know nothing about the future' than to actually do it.

In fact, that is the reason that I am writing this at all. I want the reader to know that it is possible to get knocked on your butt with devastating news and then stand up and refuse to allow circumstances to dictate how you will feel about the world. The pain, suffering, and grief are real, but there is no reason why you have to be enslaved to them.

In the end, I can make no promises save one: God is with you. Yes, your whole world might just go to hell. Things might go from bad to worse. Yes, I know this. Set aside my continued point that they might not and let us imagine that they will. What then? I believe in a God who understands the human situation. He knows our pain, our suffering, and our grief. If I can relate to you to some degree because of my own experiences, He can relate to you completely. If Christianity is true then the whole point of the thing is that God stepped into our world to endure its injustices, its sufferings, its agonies. We know how burdens are eased when others walk alongside us. There is no one that walks alongside us with more understanding than a God who has endured our agonies and walks alongside us all.

And if grief is at your door because something really final has happened... death has arrived... remember that this God I am describing wasn't content to merely be sympathetic. He wasn't satisfied to merely empathize with us. Part of His mission was to endure... and win a victory. He defeated death. Right now it is on the run. There will come a day when it will be completely abolished. There will come a day when all is set right. So, hold your head up. You have a God who understands and a God who conquers.

Post Script: God Chose *Joy*

I have laid out my reasons for choosing life but now that we have had our daughter I am sensitive to a 'reason' that we didn't think much about at the time. I have alluded to it several times already as I argued that Renny brings us a great deal of *joy*. Many parents report what amazing joy their disabled children bring them. ***Amazingly, this is true even in the most severe cases***.

It is difficult to keep this in mind while one is dealing with profound grief, but I can affirm their experience. All my children bring me joy, but there is something qualitatively different about *this* joy. It is hard to put into words. Perhaps the best I can do is to invoke the old cliché, "It is better to have loved and lost than never to have loved at all."

Let's face it. The moment we allow ourselves to love anyone we open ourselves up to the very strong likelihood that we will experience grief. The deeper the love, the deeper the grief. Our only alternative is to shut out the world and all of the people in it.

And grief is almost inevitable. If we are spared dealing with the loss of a loved one it is only because we have died first, leaving our loved ones to grieve *us*. Years might go by.

So much time might pass that we think we are immune to what happens to other people. No matter, grief will come. Who among us decides not to fall in love because of an almost certain bitter future parting? No, we forge ahead because in our most thoughtful moments we know that an ounce of joy outweighs a thousand pounds of grief and sorrow.

I know that joy. I suspect we all do, one way or another. We press on, clutching precious moments whenever we can and passing through the valley of the shadow of death when we must, only to love again.

It occurred to me that God has done, and is doing, the same thing. When the world fell into disobedience, He could have 'terminated' it. He could have started over with a 'clean slate.' He didn't. He chose instead to let the human race grow and flourish, knowing full well (better than we do) what pain and suffering we would inflict on each other- and on Him. In a sense, we were *all* born disabled. Yet, God chose life.

Why? It is not difficult to point to moments in history where grief was unbearable even by human standards. We can easily identify people *we* wish had never been born. Nonetheless, *God chose life*. Why?

It is a question and a conundrum that has perplexed thoughtful people throughout the centuries. To hard questions come hard answers. Here is an answer that is hard to bear, but I believe it is the right one.

The Christian Scriptures record the answer:

> Let us fix our eyes on Jesus, the author and perfecter of our faith, *who for the joy set before him endured the cross*, scorning its shame, and sat down at the right hand of the throne of God. (Hebrews 12:2)

What is this 'joy' that was set before Jesus? It becomes clear as one reads the New Testament that this joy is *us*. Jesus endured the cross and scorned its shame because an ounce of joy beats pain and shame, hands down. God endures mocking and insults and doubts because he knows that the joy of a relationship is more than worth it.

As the father of a child who is disabled I can affirm that the joy of relationship easily surpasses the pain, sorrow, and hardship that has accompanied it. If you can push yourself through the valley of suffering and doubt you find yourself in today I think you'll discover the same. You might also gain an insight into the heart of God. It is something to consider.

Appendix A

This book is intentionally brief and purposely avoids exploring in depth every possible ethical scenario. The resources below accentuate the purpose of the book. If you want to go even deeper than this, consider making use of the study guides available on the website: www.wechoselife.com.

Other Resources:
Books:

Freedom: Healing for Parents of Disabled Children
Author: Nancy Douglas
ISBN 9780615188225

Forever Loved: A Personal Account of Grief and Resurrection
Author: Gary Habermas
College Press Publishing Company
ISBN 9780899007960

Audio:
Job and the Problem of Evil
Eleonore Stump
http://www.veritas.org/media/talks/151

Internet:
Going to this page: www.wechoselife.com
Will give you more information about:
Spina Bifida, Cerebral Palsy, Down Syndrome, Gene Therapy, Cleft Palate, Cystic Fibrosis, Etc

Appendix B

There is a God and He Died on a Cross and Rose from the Dead

There are numerous allusions in this book to the assertion that if one believes in God then the abortion question shifts dramatically. I tried to frame the arguments in such a way that even if you don't believe in God, or are unsure, you could feel the weight of them. I said that the question of God's existence, like the abortion decision itself, is best approached before one is in 'the situation.' Still, it seemed like something might be appropriate since you might be in it right now.

People have been arguing about the existence of God for centuries. The arguments for and against have basically stayed the same. Many people are persuaded by that which seems awfully like Design. We might illustrate this by looking at the unborn child itself. It only takes one tiny deviation in the genetic code to create a birth defect- one tiny deviation out of hundreds of thousands, if not millions, of things that must go right- and usually do. Between all the things that have to happen and happen at just the right moment for the mother and all the things that have to happen and happen at just the right moment for the child, many people infer that there is really good Design here. And that's just regarding childbirth!

Such arguments are in the realm of what is called 'natural' theology, or in other words, what one might be able to learn about God without Him telling you Himself. Such an argument has limitations even if one thinks they are effective. You may decide there is a God but might not learn about the things He likes and dislikes. For that you would need what is called 'revealed' theology.

For a perfect example of the limits of an argument from the 'natural' order consider this: everyone believes that there is something that has always existed. Either they think this 'thing' is God or they think it is the universe. There isn't any intellectual advantage to saying that it is the universe as opposed to God if only for the reason that the universe, according to scientists, had a beginning. It is hard to think that something has always existed when it had a beginning. What was around before the universe if not God? No one can say. You may as well consider the possibility that it is God, who, by definition, never had a beginning, which is the thing that has always existed. This is all well and good but what have we learned about God through this exercise? Not much. Just that He has always existed and that He didn't have a beginning.

So, as much as I find these sorts of arguments useful, I believe that anything interesting we're going to learn about God is going to have to be revealed by Him. If He exists, that is. Obviously, one can't decide He doesn't exist or that it is unlikely that He exists before looking into claims throughout history of revelations allegedly by God because that would be circular reasoning.

It just so happens that there is one argument for the existence of God that combines both 'natural' and 'revealed' components and only one religion on the planet can make it. Let me offer you this as another argument for the existence of God. By the time we are done you will understand why I picked this one and why I think it is relevant to this book.

There is only one religion on the planet that says that God actually came to our planet, in person, as a human. Here is the perfect marriage of 'natural' and 'revealed.' We naturally know lots of things about humans. For example, we know that they all die. If there was a human that didn't die, we would stand up and take notice. If there was a human that died but then rose from the dead with an entirely new body we'd wait in stunned silence for an explanation. According to Christianity this is exactly what happened and the explanation that was offered was that this human was exactly who He said He was: God Himself.

Since Jesus was a human, He was seen and heard and touched by multitudes. If He was in fact God, then we have the missing component from 'natural' approaches. In Jesus, God was able to communicate what He was like and what He wanted and what He wanted to do. If Jesus really said He was God and really did rise from the dead then we have a new argument for the existence of God. It is based on whether or not the resurrection really happened. If it did, this validates Jesus' claim and you can not only be sure that God exists but also study what He said to see what kind of God He really is.

So, did Jesus really claim to be God and did He really rise from the dead? The first half of our question is answered simply enough by looking at one example from one account of Jesus' life and times, the book of John.

Again the Jews picked up stones to stone him, but Jesus said to them, "I have shown you many great miracles from the Father. For which of these do you stone Me?"

"We are not stoning You for any of these, replied the Jews, "but for blasphemy, because You, a mere man, claim to be God." John 10:31-33

It is quite clear, then, that Jesus was saying things that meant He was claiming to be God.

Did He then also rise from the dead?

There are a number of good reasons to think that He did. In the first place, it was the Jews that had Jesus put to death in the first place. The last thing they would have wanted is for people to say that He had risen from the dead. However, after Jesus' death, they never produced the body of Jesus to show that Jesus' disciples were lying about the resurrection.

In fact, the only defense the Jews could make admitted that the body of Jesus was missing! They concocted a story that the disciples stole the body while the guards were sleeping. The first thing we note, then, is that the body of Jesus is missing: the tomb is empty.

If it seems plausible to you that the

disciples could have really stolen the body right underneath the noses of so many trained guards, Roman and Jewish, it is enough to say that the people who actually lived in the area and first heard the claims were not persuaded in the slightest that this was a credible explanation. The disciples pronounced the resurrection right in the very same city in which Jesus was put to death and His body went 'missing.' More than that, it was during the Jewish Passover, which means that the city of Jerusalem had swelled in population. There would have been people everywhere, including camping in the hills, where Jesus was buried. If there was even a hint of a rumor that the disciples could actually have pulled it off, there would have been no audience for the disciples.

The next major festival was just fifty days after the Passover and again Jerusalem swells in population. Here the disciples offer their boldest declarations about Jesus, again right in the very place where Jesus died and where His body went 'missing.' The result according to the history book called Acts: three thousand people converted on the first day the message was announced. (Acts 2:40) After this, many more thousands would become Christians, too. Even if you think these numbers are inflated, remember that there were already so many Christians by around 60 AD, in Rome, a thousand or so miles away, that Nero could blame the torching of Rome on the Christians who were abundant in the city. (He coated many with tar and burned them alive to provide light for the city). What is the best explanation for so many thousands of people becoming Christians?

Finally, it isn't only that Jesus' body was missing or that His disciples were preaching the resurrection in the city where it allegedly occurred. We like to think that Jesus only appeared to the disciples. If that were the case, not only would it be hard to understand how many thousands of people converted to Christianity but it would also make us nervous, since there were only a small handful of disciples; conspiracies are better when the number of people involved are small. We are being arrogant if we think that people back then wouldn't have been suspicious, too. So what about it?

One of the oldest books we have discussing Christianity is the book of 1 Corinthians. Written by a man named Paul, it is probably even older than the written accounts of Jesus' life. In one passage, Paul says:

For what I received I passed on to you as of first importance: that Christ died for our sins according to the Scriptures, that He was buried, that He was raised on the third day according to the Scriptures, and that He appeared to Peter, and then to the Twelve. *After that He appeared to more than five hundred of the brothers at the same time*, most of whom are still living, though some have fallen asleep. Then He appeared to James, then to all the apostles, and last of all He appeared to me also, as to one abnormally born. (1 Cor. 15:3-7)

So you see, Jesus did not appear only to the disciples. According to Paul's account, in at least one incident, He appeared to five hundred people at the same time. It begins to make more sense now why so many thousands would convert in a single day and thousands more in the short time afterwards.

Sometimes, we worry about believing things that are so old but we should remember that Paul was writing his letter not more than twenty years after the death of Jesus. A lot of people would have been around to 'check him out.' It would be like making a claim about something happening twenty years before now, say during the 1980s. There are lots of people around who were alive then. The first Christians had a lot of enemies, many of whom tried to kill them. If these enemies could have refuted the story they would have. However, we do not have a single account from anyone during this time period contesting the basic factual assertions made by the Christians. Not one. Moreover, Christianity spread and spread and spread.

Perhaps you are objecting that the above is all well and good, but how can we even trust the information above? Doesn't it come from 'old books'? The truth is that much of what I have said is accepted as historical by non-Christians. This includes the existence of Jesus as a historical person, his crucifixion by Pontius Pilate, Jesus' missing body, and the wildfire spread of the Christian faith. The sole hang up for these scholars (like John Dominic Crossan) are the miraculous elements. In other words, they accept much of what I have said- just not the resurrection.

Why not? Is it because they dispute the evidence or because they have are biased against anything that might smack of the supernatural? If they accept so much of the other material, but not the miracles or resurrection, I contend that suspiciously sounds like naturalistic bias.

However, of there wasn't a real resurrection, I suggest that there remains an interesting historical problem to resolve. How did the Christians convince so many in so short a time in the face of such violent opposition? They weren't paying people money to believe. They weren't threatening people with death- evangelism with a sword. Christianity didn't become the 'state' religion until almost three hundred years after the resurrection is said to have happened. Those three hundred years contained numerous bloody assaults on Christianity and yet the faith grew and grew. How do we account for this- especially if there was no resurrection?

If we lay aside assumption and focus on the evidence, I suggest that the best explanation, from the historical records, is that Jesus really did rise from the dead.

What is the value and relevance of this approach? Why do we bother with it at the end of a book urging people not to abort their children? Well, I said that if Jesus really was God and we had a good reason to believe it, then we can learn more about God's thoughts by hearing what Jesus had to say. Jesus had some things to say, indeed!

Consider one of the most famous passages

of the Bible, Jesus tells a Pharisee:

> For God so loved the world that He gave His one and only Son, that whoever believes in Him shall not perish but have eternal life. (John 3:16).

There are two things we can note. In the first place, Jesus contends that God loves the *entire* world. God cares about all people. He makes no distinction between young and old, male or female- or born or unborn. Jesus died for all people in all ages. He died for us today even though we weren't even born yet!

It is difficult to believe in God in Christ and not recognize that it is God who decides the value of a person and personhood can't be reduced to physical factors such as our developmental age, since God sacrificed His Son while we weren't any age at all!

There is another important point. This passage demonstrates that Jesus was deeply sympathetic to the plight of man and had every intention of doing something about it. It may be a mystery why He hasn't done anything *yet*, but it can't be said He is indifferent to our situation.

This is highlighted in another incident described in the New Testament. Jesus is informed that his friend, Lazarus, is very sick. Jesus delays his coming until in fact Lazarus dies. When Jesus arrives he is immersed in the sorrow and grief of those who loved Lazarus. In the meantime, Jesus already knows what he is going to do. He knows that he is going to bring Lazarus back to life. Despite knowing this, despite knowing that he has the power over death itself, Jesus is moved. In the shortest verse in the Bible we read: "Jesus wept." (John 11:35)

It is so easy to look at our universe and perceive that God is utterly indifferent to our circumstances. Yet in Jesus we learn otherwise. The truth is that God cares about us. *That's the whole reason why He came.* He came to defeat sin, death, and the devil, and He paid a price with His own blood to accomplish it. He knows what it is like to suffer and grieve. He saw death in His own life and mourned it. He suffered death... but overcame it.

If this is all true, consider what it means to our situation, then. However much we feel like we are alone, however bad the news is, however torturous the decision before us, God knows and understands. More than that, He says that He plans on coming again to make things right. It is certainly hard in the meantime, but if He kept His word the first time, He will keep His word the second time.

What I say is not true because it is comforting, but is comforting because it is true. No other 'religion' offers a consolation like this one. I strongly urge you to consider the matter for yourself. If you discover that it is true that God is present in your pain, then you know that He is aware of your unborn child's predicament. However hard it is to understand why He would allow such painful things to continue, we know that He has a reason for allowing it. We don't have to know that reason. What is important is that He knows that reason and in the meantime, weeps for our pain right to the present moment. He will give you strength to face this present moment. You don't know what the future holds. You can't. Put your trust in God today and receive strength for enduring the problems of today.

He'll take care of tomorrow.

For further reading about the fact of the Resurrection and the truth of Christianity the following books are recommended:

The Historical Jesus: Ancient Evidence for The Life of Christ
>Author: Gary Habermas
>College Press Publishing Company
>ISBN 978-0899007328

The Son Rises: The Historical Evidence for the Resurrection of Jesus.
>Author: William Lane Craig
>Wipf & Stock Publishers
>ISBN 978-1579104641

Mere Christianity
>Author: C.S. Lewis
>Touchstone Books
>ISBN 978-0684823782

Anthony is available to speak at churches, schools and other organizations. He is also willing to speak directly to parents struggling with issues related to the topics covered in this book.

>You may contact him at:
>author@wechoselife.com

>www.wechoselife.com

NOTES:

NOTES:

www.ingramcontent.com/pod-product-compliance
Lightning Source LLC
Chambersburg PA
CBHW071421040426
42445CB00012BA/1233